An Hachette UK Company
www.hachette.co.uk

First published in Great Britain in 2015 by Ticktock,
an imprint of Octopus Publishing Group Ltd
Endeavour House
189 Shaftesbury Avenue
London
WC2H 8JY
www.octopusbooks.co.uk
www.ticktockbooks.co.uk

ISBN 978 1 78325 237 4

A CIP record for this book is available from the British Library.

Printed and bound in China

1 3 5 7 9 10 8 6 4 2

Text by Anna Bowles   Design by Clare Barber
Managing Editor: Karen Rigden
Production Controller: Sarah-Jayne Johnson

Pictures Credits
Every effort has been made to trace the copyright holders, and we apologise in advance for
any unintentional omissions. We would be pleased to insert the appropriate
acknowledgement in any subsequent edition of this publication.
Acknowledgements in Source Order
a = above, b = below, c = centre, l = left, r = right, bg = background, m = main

Fotolia Dario Sabljak 22 b; Snowshill 47 m; XYZproject 19 b;

Getty Images 123render 38 bl; AFP/ Stringer 36 c; Barcroft Media 24 l, 26 ac;
David Trood 35 a; Ed Norton 34 bl, Erik Dreyer 48 br; Gareth Cattermole 26 b;
Thomas Northcut 40 c; VisitBritain/Daniel Bosworth 46 b;

istockphoto.com Aneese 26 bc; Atypeek 9 bg, 28 l; cjp 31 m;
designalldone 16 bl, 16 c, 16 AR, 17 bl, 17 a; emuemu 12 c; irakite 24 r;
John_ Woodcock 29 m; KreangchaiRungfama 25 m; MGSmith 42 b;
siartmailru 1 c, 3 a; SpiffyJ 13 bg;

Shutterstock ExpressVectors 34 bg; HS3RUS 38 bg; Luca
Villanova 39 m; 9lives 2 bg, 14 bg,16 bg, 18 bg, 20 bg, 22 bg, 48 bg;
Bard Sandemose 23 al, Bloom Design15 b, 15 ac, David P. Lewis 43 al,
44 m; Designua17 br; ExpressVectors 32 bg, 36 bg, GalaStudio 15 c;
hans engbers 27 cr; HS3RUS 40 bg; judilyn, 32 ar, 33 ar, 35 br, 37 b,
37 cr, 38 ar, 41 ar, 41 ac, 48 ar, 48 acr; Magnia 42 bg, 44 bg, 46 bg;
Mark Grenier 5 bg, 6 bg, 7 acl, 7 b, 8 bg, 10 bg, 12 bg; Olga
Drozdova 23 bl; Paul McKinnon 43 br; troyka 24 bg, 26 bg, 28 bg, 30 bg;

Thinkstock '3c43f815_774' 22 cr; artist_arefin 3 bl, 33 a; David Spieth 5 ar;
esenkartal 34 c; Heiko Küverling 40 bc; Joachim Angeltun 10 c;
Juriah Mosin 28 br; Kannaa11 bg; LucasRidley 36 l; m-gucci 32 b; michael ledray
34 ar; Paul Fleet 18 b,18 a,18 bc, 20 c; Pavel Khorenyan 3 br, 14 ar, 14 bc;
rep0rter 41 al; somkcr 4 cb; Thomas Northcut 41 c; Valerijs Kostins 8 c; william87 33 br.

Contents

Popping and Pulsing

Are your eyes throbbing yet?

Amazing optical illusions like this one take advantage of the shift between what your eyes see and what your brain perceives. Your brain is being fooled by the way your eyes process information!

Some scientists think that when you stare at a point such as the white circle in the centre of this image, your eyes jitter slightly, so that they report movement in nearby objects when they are actually still. Another theory is that when you glance around the image, motion detectors in your brain get confused and report that they are seeing movement.

THE JURY'S OUT ON WHICH OF THESE THEORIES IS TRUE, BUT EITHER WAY,

THE RESULTS ARE TRULY MIND-MUDDLING.

Oodles of Illusions

WORK THOSE EYEBALLS!

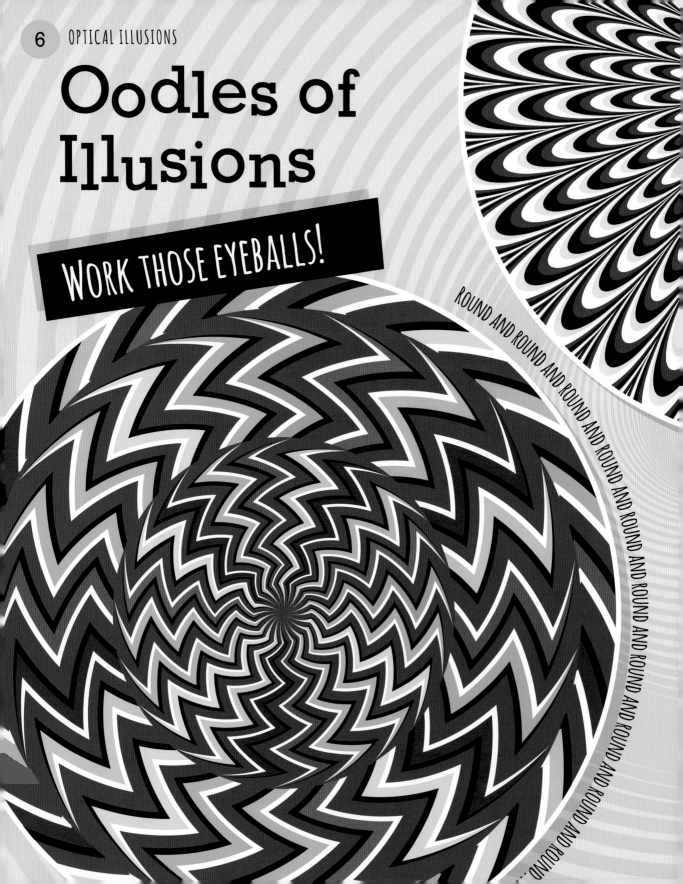

ROUND AND ROUND AND ROUND AND ROUND AND ROUND AND ROUND AND ROUND AND ROUND AND ROUND AND ROUND AND ROUND AND ROUND AND ROUND AND ROUND ...

Optical illusions come in different colours and different shapes, but the one thing they have in common is repetition. That's probably what confuses the brain the most, as it reports several very similar lines close together, gets them mixed up and perceives them to be moving.

SPECTACULAR SPECS!

YOU'D SEE QUITE A SPECTACLE.

Swarming Squares

It's not just curves that get in on the action.
This illusion uses squares for a similar effect to
the concentric circles on the previous page.

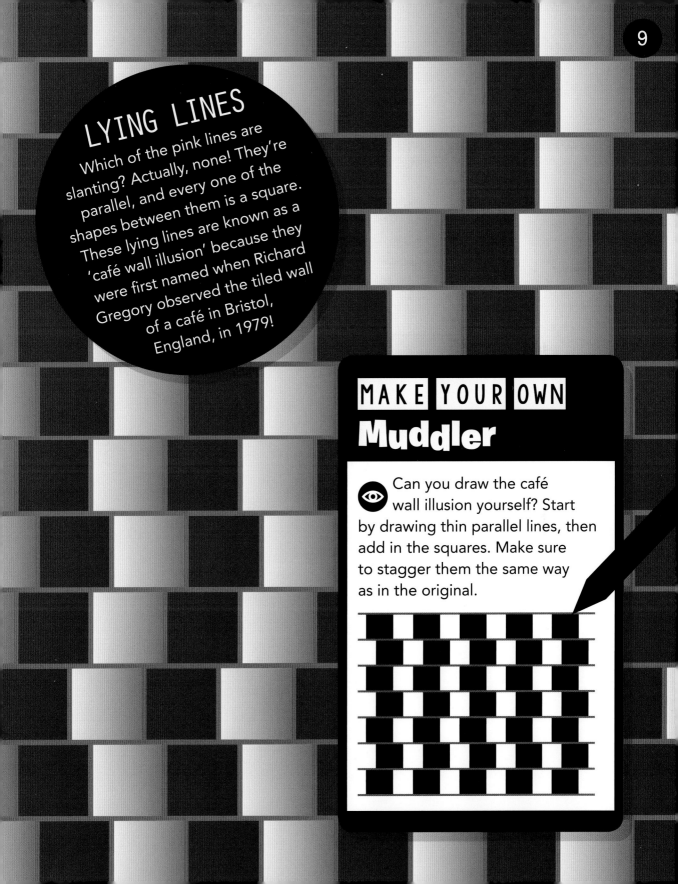

LYING LINES

Which of the pink lines are slanting? Actually, none! They're parallel, and every one of the shapes between them is a square. These lying lines are known as a 'café wall illusion' because they were first named when Richard Gregory observed the tiled wall of a café in Bristol, England, in 1979!

MAKE YOUR OWN
Muddler

Can you draw the café wall illusion yourself? Start by drawing thin parallel lines, then add in the squares. Make sure to stagger them the same way as in the original.

Deceptive Depth

COULD YOU JUMP RIGHT

INTO THIS PAGE?

⬆ This image consists of simple curved lines printed on
the flat page. It looks like a tunnel because of the way
the white curves use different shades of grey.

BOGUS BULGE

⬆ That's not a photograph of a pillow, but a computer-generated flat image. The lines between the dots gradually get curvier and curvier as your eye moves out from the centre of the image, and the dots get more oval as if you were seeing them at an angle. Because that's what a 3D object looks like, your brain assumes that a 3D object is what it's seeing!

Innies OR Outies?

Are the middle corners of the purple cubes poking outwards? Or the middle corners of the blue cubes? Or both? Or what or which…? It's confusing!

IN, OUT, SHAKE IT ALL ABOUT!

STARTING BLOCKS

The most basic cube illusions only use three shades of a single colour, like this one.

TRY TURNING YOUR BOOK UPSIDE DOWN.

OF THE CUBES, YOU SEE AS THE TOP?

DOES THAT AFFECT WHICH SIDE

MAKE YOUR OWN
Muddler

If you've got enough different felt-tip pens, cube illusions are easy to draw. You just have to make sure that you use three different shades for each cube, and always use the same shade in the same place on each cube. The illusion opposite uses purple, green and blue – can you create a cube illusion in red, pink and orange? Or just use three shades of red to create a version of the image shown here.

Endless Paradox

This fake 3D arrangement is called a Penrose triangle. In this example, shading is again used to create the impression of cubes. But this time they're arranged in what appear to be three rows.

Remove the three middle cubes from any one of the three sides of the triangle and what's left will stop looking impossible. Hold your thumb over the page to see!

MAKE YOUR OWN
Muddler

You can easily draw a Penrose triangle by following these instructions.

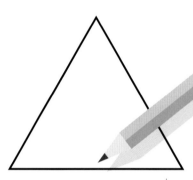

1 Using a pencil, draw an equilateral triangle (one where all the sides are the same length).

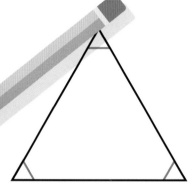

2 Add lines at the points to create three small, identical equilateral triangles.

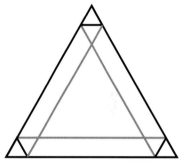

3 Draw straight lines between the inside tips of the small triangles.

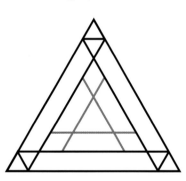

4 Draw two lines across the central triangle as shown.

5 Rub out the lines shown in grey to leave your perfect Penrose triangle.

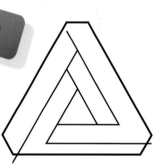

6 Why not colour in your Mind Muddler?

TIP: USE A RULER!

Tangled Teasers

PENROSE TRIANGLE

You've met the Penrose triangle...

now meet the Escher's cube

and the Mobius strip.

ESCHER'S CUBE

MOBIUS STRIP

⬆ All these shapes are created by drawing simple two-dimensional lines in a way that tricks the brain into seeing three dimensions.

Here are a couple more impossible shapes that work on the same principle:

PROLIFERATING PENROSES!

ANOTHER KIND OF ESCHER'S CUBOID

MAKE YOUR OWN
Muddler

There's no such thing as a Mobius strip in nature – but you can make one in a few seconds! Just get a strip of paper, twist it once and tape the ends together. Hey presto, an endless loop of paper with only one side.

Boggling Buildings

Impossible objects can be really simple, or amazingly complicated. Here are some cool computer-generated examples.

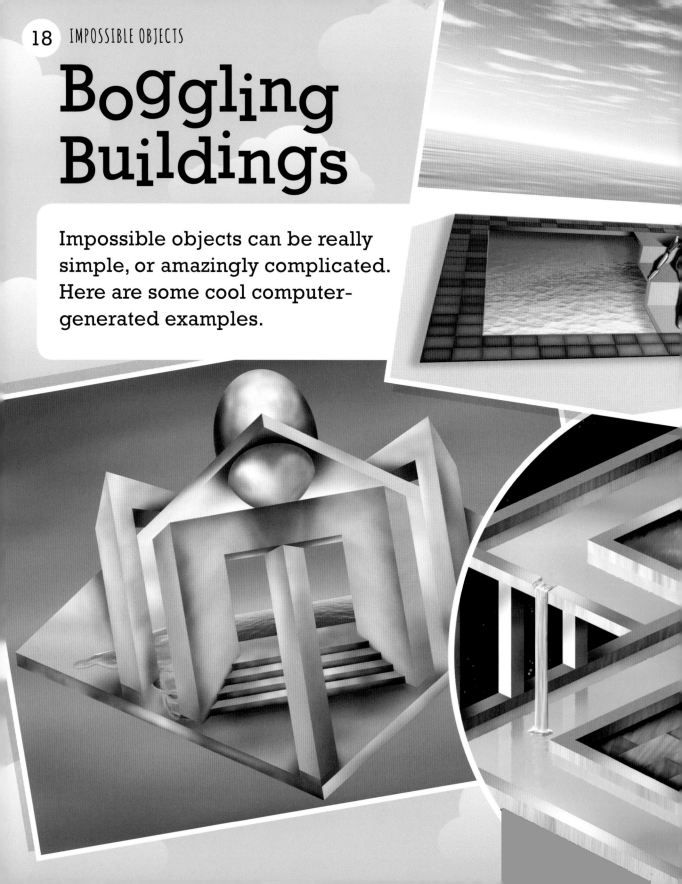

Can you see how the shapes on the previous page underlie these computer creations?

The Blinding Blivet

A blivet is an optical illusion that looks a bit like a fork – but you wouldn't want to eat your dinner with one of these.

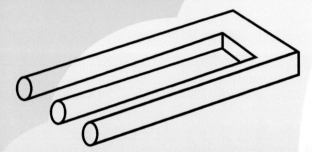

THE BLIVET IS THE BASIS OF A LOT OF

ILLUSIONARY BUILDINGS,

LIKE THE SET OF COLUMNS ON THE RIGHT.

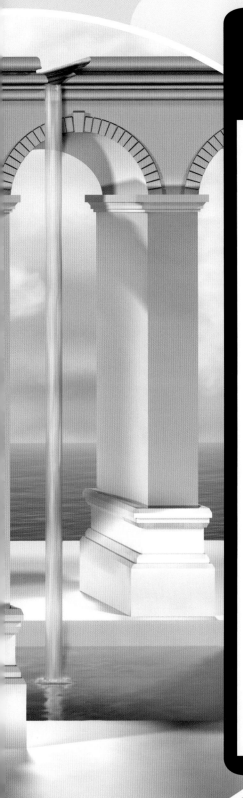

MAKE YOUR OWN
Muddler

Follow these simple steps to draw a blivet yourself.

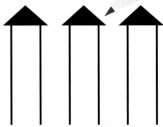

1 Draw six evenly spaced 10cm lines.

2 Give each pair of lines a 'hat'. It could be any shape you fancy, this example uses triangles.

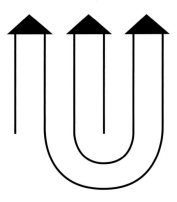
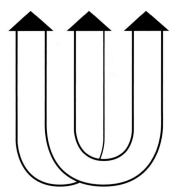

3 Draw a curved line connecting the second and sixth lines. Connect the third and fifth lines in the same way. Keep your lines as smooth and tidy as you can.

4 To complete the blivet you need to draw a half curve from the first line, stopping as it hits the other curve, then leave a gap before continuing to meet up with the fourth line.

Terrific Tessellations

A brick pavement is a perfect tessellation, but not a very exciting one. You can make shapes that are much more interesting. Like these!

A TESSELLATION IS A REPEATED SHAPE

THAT COVERS A FLAT SURFACE

WITHOUT LEAVING ANY GAPS.

The more you look at a tessellation, the more you'll start to see other patterns and movement. What can you see in these t-shirt designs?

ARE YOUR EYES BOGGLED YET?

Tessellation is often used on fabric prints to create a striking effect.

MAKE YOUR OWN
Muddler

👁 You can create a tessellating shape by starting with an equilateral triangle and altering each side in the same way.

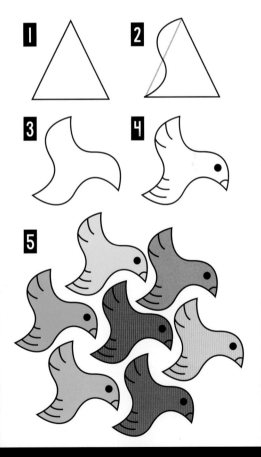

1

2

3

4

5

Illusions Underfoot

Amazing 3D pavement art creates the impression of the ground opening up.

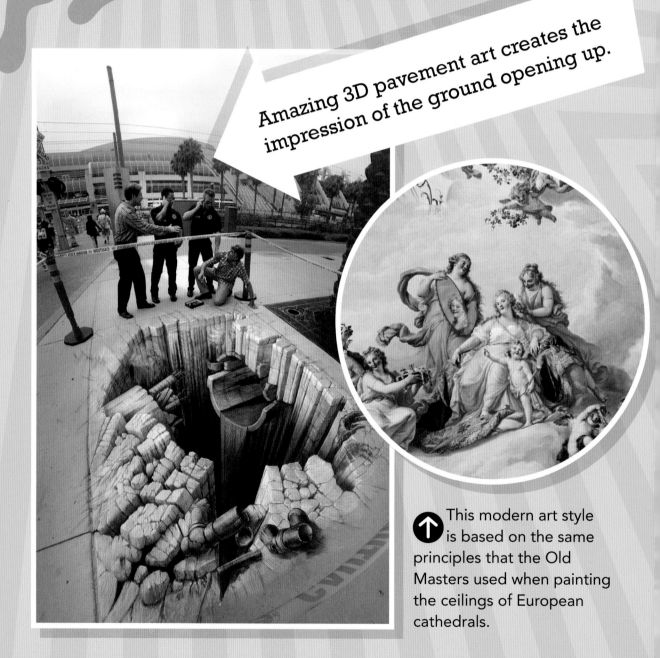

⬆ This modern art style is based on the same principles that the Old Masters used when painting the ceilings of European cathedrals.

If you looked at this kind of street art from directly above, it would appear strange and distorted. But viewed from ground level as you walk by, it looks absolutely real. Everything is drawn at an oblique angle that imitates the way you see things that really are three dimensional.

Street Smart

HERE'S SOME MORE

INCREDIBLE 3D STREET ART.

Examples of 3D street art from around the world. The one on the top left was the world's largest 3D painting, created in London in 2011. It measured over 1,120 square metres.

Seeing Double

Do you know the famous glass and faces illusion?
Is it two people, or an elegant goblet?

IT COMES IN A NUMBER

OF VARIATIONS, TOO.

THE KNOW-HOW

← The glass and faces image is referred to as a figure/ground illusion. In this kind of illusion, one single line forms the edge of two different shapes at the same time. Your brain interprets objects by working out where their contours (edges) are, so when it sees a line that looks like a contour, it sees an object. But it knows a contour can only belong to one object, so you can only see either the glass or the faces at any one time.

Double Duos

Another kind of double drawing is a face that looks like one person one way up, and another person the other way up, like this image of a princess and her stepmother.

AND THEN THERE ARE DRAWINGS THAT LOOK LIKE TWO THINGS.

← Is it an old lady staring off to the left, or a young lady looking over her shoulder?

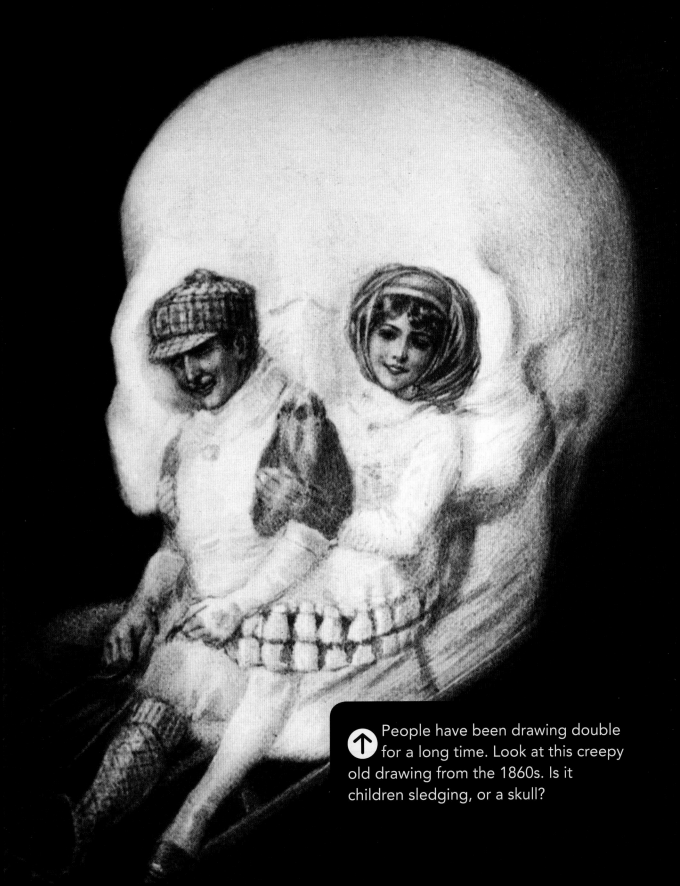

People have been drawing double for a long time. Look at this creepy old drawing from the 1860s. Is it children sledging, or a skull?

Deceptive Distances

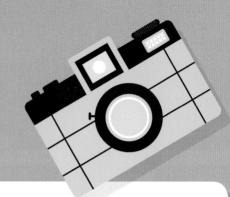

Forced perspective is the name for what happens when you take a photograph of a large, distant object next to a small, close one. If you're careful to avoid overlapping the two, they can look like they're right next to each other.

THE KNOW-HOW

Forced perspective photographs work because your brain assumes everything it's seeing is on the same scale. A good forced perspective image will probably have just one tiny object and one huge one on a plain background – like the woman with the Leaning Tower of Pisa. The photograph of the man and the sun doesn't work quite so well because of the different tones and shades in the sky. The man is lit in a different way to the sky, so that clues your brain in to the fact that he's not in the same place.

Forcing the Issue

Here are some more simple but amazing uses of forced perspective. Can you set up similar photos with your family and friends?

↙ This image isn't actually forced perspective but it works in a similar way to create the impression of something impossible. Because the boy bending over and the boy in the sand are in proportion with one another, your mind puts the two together.

MAKE YOUR OWN
Muddler

👁 You don't need the Leaning Tower of Pisa or the Golden Gate Bridge to create a forced perspective image. Just take your camera to the park and find a leaning tree!

Deceptive Danglers

There are other ways to create photos that trick the mind and boggle the imagination. How about just hanging around?

← This man is, of course, lying on a flat road surface, but he's posing as if he was dangling. There is nothing in the image – such as a manhole or a plant – that tells us he isn't hanging vertically.

MAKE YOUR OWN
Muddler

You probably don't need our guidance on how to set up simple versions of these photos. However, do not lie down in the middle of the road! If a car comes along you'll be in more than a muddle.

Artist Leandro Erlich created 'Dalston House' in London, England in 2013. This was a full façade of a terraced house, built on the ground with a large mirror above it to reflect people dangling from the structure!

Tilt Shift...

LOOK AT THIS AMAZING MODEL OF FLORENCE CATHEDRAL.

And now look again, when we tell you it's not a model at all! This cool miniaturisation effect is achieved by a camera trick called 'tilt shift'.

IT LOOKS LIKE YOU COULD PICK IT UP!

MAKE YOUR OWN
Muddler

Some cameras are equipped with a tilt-shift lens, which simulates a shallow depth of field (this creates some blurred and some super-sharp areas in your photograph). It helps to be high up as this adds to the illusion of looking down at a model.

Or if you don't fancy buying an expensive camera and hanging out of a helicopter, lots of apps are available which will create the effect on your own photos. Why not snap the view from an upstairs window, feed it into a tilt shift generator and see what happens?

FLORENCE CATHEDRAL – NOT A MODEL!

Diddy Dioramas

Here are some of the amazing results you can get with tilt-shift photography.

ALL OF THESE ARE REAL BUILDINGS, VEHICLES AND PEOPLE!

The Art of Balance

ROCK BALANCING, ANYONE?

It doesn't sound like a hot trend, but rock balancing can produce some very cool results such as this example in Sausalito, California. These sculptures were created at the beach, and left there for people to admire.

THE KNOW-HOW

👁 Nope, there are no wires, glue or hidden supports. Balancers select rocks that have just the right weight and shape to counterbalance each other, and take advantage of natural features like grooves in the stone surface to act as a socket for the next rock in the pile. It can take hours to locate and arrange just the right rocks, but it's worth it.

➡ The beach is probably the best place for finding a large number of interestingly shaped rocks. But you might also get lucky in any wild place such as a wood or a hillside.

Defying Gravity

Check out these amazing examples
of the art of rock balancing.

THERE'S EVEN AN ANNUAL INTERNATIONAL STONE BALANCE FESTIVAL IN OTTAWA, CANADA. HERE'S EXPERT BALANCER DAN DAVIS AT WORK AT THE FESTIVAL.

MAKE YOUR OWN
Muddler

 This one requires a steady hand and lots of patience. Get an adult to help you and don't build them too high as they can easily topple over and hurt you – squished toes are best avoided!

1 Find the right surface for your rock sculpture to stand on. Ideally your bottom rock will rest in slight indentations on the surface that match the rock's underside.

2 Rocks come in a lot of different types. You don't have to be an expert geologist to use this fact – just pay attention to their textures and weights.

3 It's actually easier to balance larger rocks than smaller ones, because heavy rocks have more weight and stability.

Going Green

When is grass not just a plant? When it's the hair on a giant head rising up out of the ground!

→ These sculptures from the Lost Gardens of Heligan in Cornwall are called the Green Giant and the Mud Maiden. They were created by Victorian landscape designers, then forgotten for a hundred years until they were rediscovered in 1990.

MAKE YOUR OWN
Muddler

👁 It'll take some time, but if you have a garden you could create your own Green Giant, or perhaps a Green Dwarf if space is limited. Why not start by painting a face on a pebble and planting grass to grow around one side as hair? If you don't have a garden try using cress and growing it on your windowsill.

The Endless Selfie

And finally here's the ultimate Make Your Own Muddler. Anyone with a tablet and a mirror can recreate this eye-twister.

→ Start by taking a picture of your face on the tablet. With the photo set to full screen, stand in front of the mirror and hold the tablet in front of your face, then snap another picture. With this second photo set to full screen, hold it in front of your face again and take another shot. Keep on snapping in this way and see how many versions of yourself you can get into one image.

CAN YOU BEAT THE

FIVE IN THE PICTURE?